I'M STILL IMPORTANT!

WAYLAND

NEW EXPERIENCES

I Want That Room! – Moving house
I'm Still Important! – A new baby
Open Wide! – My first trip to the dentist
Where's My Peg? – My first day at school

Published in Great Britain in 2000 by Hodder Wayland,
an imprint of Hodder Children's Books
This edition published in 2007 by Wayland,
an imprint of Hachette Children's Books,
an Hachette UK Company,
www.hachette.co.uk
Reprinted in 2009 by Wayland

Editor: Jason Hook
Designer: Tessa Barwick
Cover Designer: Caroline Martin

A Catalogue record for this book is available from the British Library.

ISBN 978 0 7502 5280 5

Printed and bound in China

Hachette Children's Books
338 Euston Road, London NW1 3BH
www.hachette.co.uk

I'M STILL IMPORTANT!

A new baby

Written by Jen Green

Illustrated by Mike Gordon

WAYLAND

When I was helping Mum in the garden, she told me a secret.

'I'm expecting a new baby, Rachel,' she said. 'Soon you'll have a little brother or sister.'

5

Mum's bump got bigger and bigger. 'The baby is growing inside my tummy,' she said.

'Can you feel the baby moving?'

I helped Mum and Dad get the nursery ready. I sorted out some of my old toys. Then, I helped choose the baby's name.

Mum and Dad were very excited.
I was excited too, but I also felt
a bit worried.

Would the new baby want to
share my food ...

... or play with
all my toys?

'Will you still love me when the baby is born?' I asked Dad.

He gave me a big hug, and said: 'Of course we will. You'll always be our special Rachel.'

When Mum and Dad went to hospital to have the baby, Gran came to look after me.

Then Dad phoned. 'Great news, Rachel,' he said. 'You've got a baby brother!' Gran was excited.

Next day, we visited Mum in hospital. She gave me a big hug.

I peeped at the new baby.
He opened his eyes and
seemed to smile at me.

Soon Mum and Dad came home with Harry.

All their friends came over.
Someone said Harry looked
like me when I was a baby.

Harry didn't do much at first.
He mostly cried or slept, but
he did like to be cuddled.

Sometimes I wished I was small again, so Mum would cuddle me like that.

One day, Mum and I were busy playing when Harry started crying.

I felt cross. 'You never have time to play now,' I said. 'You don't love me as much now Harry's here!'

I'm still IMPORTANT!

'We love you more than ever!' said Mum. 'But Harry needs us a lot just now, because he's so small.'

When Dad came home, Mum played just with me.

26

Harry needed a lot of looking after.
Sometimes I helped to bath him.

To make Harry laugh,
I pulled faces ...

I made noises ...

and I played games.

27

Harry was small at first,
but he is growing quickly.

Harry can crawl, and we're teaching him to walk. Now we are a bigger family, we have even more fun.

Notes for parents and teachers

This book introduces children to the experience of a new baby in the family. Parents or teachers may find it useful to stop and discuss issues with children as they come up in the text.

A new baby brings major changes for all family members, not least young children. New challenges may include practical matters such as finding out about a baby's needs and how to help deal with them, and emotional issues such as how to cope with change.

If a new baby is expected in the family, your child may well feel anxious. Encourage him or her to talk about feelings. Be honest and admit that the new baby will bring changes. Encourage your child to look forward to the new experience by stressing the positive aspects of having a new baby brother or sister.

This book describes a number of different reactions to a new baby. Children may feel proud and excited about the new arrival. They may also feel insecure, left out, bored, jealous, or a mixture of all these. They may react by becoming difficult, angry, demanding, withdrawn or more babyish. It is hard to come to terms with having to share parents' attention, and not coming first all the time. Talking about feelings nearly always helps. Parents with new babies should try to set aside special time for their older children.

Reread the story, encouraging children to take the role of different characters. Ask children with new brothers and sisters to talk about their own experiences and feelings. How do these experiences differ from those described in the book?

The book also shows a cat having kittens. Discuss animal babies, drawing on children's experiences of pets.

Encourage children to find out about their own birth and babyhood. They might like to make a 'birthday book' which could include photographs, drawings, and family memories of their first year. Children might like to bring in photographs of themselves as babies. These could be pinned up on a wall and children invited to guess the identity of the babies.

The experience of a new baby may introduce children to a number of unfamiliar words, including womb, pregnancy, expecting, clinic, scan, check-up, maternity ward, midwife, delivery, breast-feeding, teething. Make a list of new words and explain what they mean.

Use this book for teaching literacy

This book can help you in the literacy hour in the following ways:

✓ Children can write simple stories linked to personal experience using the language of the text in this book as a model for their own writing. (Year 1, Term 3: Non-fiction writing composition.)

✓ Children can look through the book and try to locate verbs with past and present tense endings. (Year 1, Term 3: Word recognition, graphic knowledge and spelling.)

✓ The use of speech bubbles shows a different way of presenting text. (Year 2, Term 2: Sentence construction and punctuation.)

Books to read

How Do I Feel About: Our New Baby by Sarah Lavete (Franklin Watts, 1999)
Dean, Rosie, Max and May are classmates. Dean and Rosie's mums are both expecting babies. The four friends discuss their feelings and the changes that the new babies will bring.

There's a House Inside My Mummy by Giles Andreae (Orchard Books, 2002).
Looks at the arrival of a new baby in the family from a child's perspectiv
Uses rhymes and pictures to ensure children can access and undestand th
information in a humorous way.

Good Girl, Gracie Growler by Hilda Offen (Puffin Books, 1997).
Gracie Growler has a new baby brother. Everyone seems to love the new baby, but no one seems to notice Gracie any more.